D1712481

Primary Sources of American Symbols™

# The White House

Jennifer Silate

The Rosen Publishing Group's
PowerKids Press™

Published in 2006 by The Rosen Publishing Group, Inc.
29 East 21st Street, New York, NY 10010

Editor: Eric Fein
Book Design: Michael DeLisio
Photo Researcher: Amy Feinberg

Photo Credits: cover © Eyewire: American Icons; p. 4 (left) The Library Company of Philadelphia, (right) White House Historical Association (White House Collection); p. 7 (bottom) The Maryland Historical Society, Baltimore, MD, (top) Courtesy of the Massachusetts Historical Society; pp.8, 12 (left) Library of Congress Prints and Photographs Division; pp.11, 12 (right) Library of Congress; p. 15 Abbie Rowe/National Park Service; pp. 16 (left), 20 (left) Getty Images; p. 16 (right) © AP/Wide World Photos; p. 19 © Bettmann/Corbis; p. 20 (right) © Royalty-Free/Corbis

First Edition

Library of Congress Cataloging-in-Publication Data

Silate, Jennifer.
    The White House / Jennifer Silate.— 1st ed.
    p. cm. — (Primary sources of American symbols)
    Includes index.
    Contents: A home for the president — Building the president's house — The War of 1812 — Technology in the White House — Home improvements — Repairing the White house — Inside the White House — Leaving their mark — The people's house.
    ISBN 1-4042-2695-8 (lib. bdg.)
    1.  White House (Washington, D.C.)—Juvenile literature. 2.  White House (Washington, D.C.)—History—Juvenile literature. 3.  Washington (D.C.)—Buildings, structures, etc.—Juvenile literature. 4.  Presidents—United States—History—Juvenile literature. [1. White House (Washington, D.C.) 2. Presidents.] I. Title. II. Series: Silate, Jennifer.  Primary sources of American symbols.

F204.W5S66 2006
975.3—dc22
                                    2003023218

Manufactured in the United States of America

# Contents

James Hoban came to the United States from Ireland after the American Revolutionary War. From 1793 to 1802, Hoban was one of the people in charge of building the U.S. Capitol.

*Washington, in the Territory of Columbia.*

## A PREMIUM

OF 500 dollars, or a medal of that value, at the option of the party, will be given by the Commissioners of the Federal Buildings to the person who, before the fifteenth day of July next, shall produce to them the most approved plan, if adopted by them, for a President's house to be erected in this city. The site of the building, if the artist will attend to it, will of course influence the aspect and outline of his plan, and it's destination will point out to him the number, size, and distribution of the apartments. It will be a recommendation of any plan, if the central part of it may be detached and erected for the present, with the appearance of a complete whole, and be capable of admitting the additional parts, in future, if they shall be wanting. Drawings will be expected of the ground plats, elevations of each front, and sections through the building in such directions as may be necessary to explain the internal structure; and an estimate of the cubic feet of brickwork, composing the whole mass of the walls.          THE COMMISSIONERS.

# A Home for the President

The White House has been the home of the president of the United States of America for more than 200 years. In this time, the White House has become an important **symbol** of the American presidency—and of America.

Before 1791, there was no official United States capital and no official home for the president. In 1791, President George Washington chose a 10-square-mile (25.9 sq. km.) area of land to be the capital of the United States. This land was offered by the state of Maryland. The city was named Washington, District of Columbia (D.C.). In 1792, a **contest** was held to **design** the president's house, which would be located in this new city. James Hoban, an Irish-born **architect**, won the contest. Hoban won $500 for his winning design.

*This ad announces the contest calling for designs of the White House. This ad ran in Philadelphia's* National Gazette *on March 22, 1792.*

# Building the President's House

Construction of the White House began on October 13, 1792. The stone that was used for the White House came from Virginia. Construction workers lived in nearby huts that were built especially for them. On November 1, 1800, President John Adams moved into the unfinished White House. His wife, Abigail, joined him shortly after. The White House cost $272,372 to build. It was the first public building to be finished in Washington, D.C. It would also remain the largest house in the United States for about the next 70 years. The White House and its grounds take up an area of about 18 acres (7.3 hectares).

*This drawing of the White House was done by James Hoban. It shows the north face of the building. Hoban based part of his design for the White House on a large country house in Dublin, Ireland, called Leinster House.*

President John Adams wrote this letter to his wife, Abigail. In the letter, Adams tells his wife of his first night in the White House and the people with whom he met. He also tells her that he is happy she will be joining him soon at the White House.

This picture shows the burning of Washington, D.C., by British troops. Many people who lived there fled the city before the British arrived.

# The War of 1812

The United States went to war with England in 1812. During the war, the White House was almost completely destroyed by British troops. On August 24, 1814, the British entered Washington, D.C., and set fire to the White House and other buildings. Only the outer stone walls of the White House survived the fire. After the war, many members of the U.S. government wanted to move the capital to another city. President James Madison, however, wanted to rebuild Washington, D.C. **Congress** agreed. James Hoban was asked to **restore** the White House, making it look as it had before the fire. Hoban even reused some of the original stone walls. To save time, he used wood instead of brick in many parts of the building. The White House was finished by 1817.

*The White House was nearly destroyed by the fire set by British troops. After the fire was put out, only the outer walls of the White House remained standing.*

# Technology in the White House

Some of the things we take for granted in our homes had not yet been **invented** when the White House was built. Running water was added to the White House in 1833. In 1848, gaslights were placed in the building. Before then, the White House had been lit only by candles. The first telephone was put in the White House in 1879. This **technology** was so new that the White House's phone number was "1"! In 1891, another new technology was added to the White House—electricity. President Benjamin Harrison was so afraid of being hurt by the electricity, he would not turn on the lights! Throughout the years, new inventions and technologies have continued to change life in the White House.

*The electricity for the White House was supplied by a generator. This machine was stored in the nearby State, War, and Navy building. Wires attached to the generator were run into the White House. This provided power for the lights.*

The first president to have a telephone in the White House was Rutherford B. Hayes. This picture shows telephones in the executive offices in about 1890.

*This photograph from about 1846, is believed to be one of the first ever taken of the White House.*

# Home Improvements

The White House has had several different names since it was first built. In the 1800s, it was called the President's House and, later, the Executive Mansion. In 1901, it was officially named the White House by President Theodore Roosevelt. President Roosevelt made many changes to the White House during his time in office. He doubled the size of the White House's living space. In 1902, he added an office building to the house in which he and his staff worked. This building is known as the West Wing. In 1934, his cousin, President Franklin Delano Roosevelt, added another level to the West Wing. He also reconstructed the East Wing of the White House.

*This photograph shows the West Wing of the White House. In 1909, President William Howard Taft had the president's office moved into the center of the West Wing and shaped like an oval. Taft did this so he could be in the center of the day-to-day activities of his staff.*

# Repairing the White House

All of the construction **additions** added a lot of weight to the White House. When President Harry Truman moved into the building in 1945, he saw large cracks in the walls. The White House appeared to be in danger of falling down! In 1949, workers started fixing the White House. Most of the inside of the White House had to be removed. The Trumans moved to Blair House, across the street from the White House.

Wooden beams were replaced with steel to help the White House hold the weight of the additions. **Concrete** was poured under the outside stone walls to give them support. In 1952, the Trumans moved back into the White House.

*This photograph from May 17, 1950, shows the White House undergoing major construction. The inside of the building was torn down so that new, stronger walls and floors could be built.*

This photograph shows cracks in the north brick wall of the West Sitting Hall.

This photograph shows President George W. Bush meeting with his staff in the Oval Office. In the photograph, a presidential rug can be seen.

# Inside the White House

The White House is 168 feet (51.2 m) long and 152 feet (46.3 m) wide. It has 132 rooms. Each room has its own purpose. The largest room is the East Room. It is 79 feet (24 m) long and more than 36 feet (10.9 m) wide. The East Room is used to hold large parties. The Blue Room is the room where the president greets people who come to visit. The president's office is the Oval Office, which is in the West Wing. The office is called the Oval Office because it is in the shape of an **oval**. The president often gives speeches from his desk in the Oval Office. These speeches are seen on television around the world.

*In this photograph, President William Jefferson Clinton and his wife, Hillary Rodham Clinton dance in front of guests in the East Room. The Clintons were hosting a dinner for the National Governors Association.*

# Leaving Their Mark

Each president who has lived in the White House made additions to the building during his term. First Ladies, or presidents' wives, have also worked on making changes to the White House. In 1961, Jacqueline Kennedy, President John F. Kennedy's wife, worked on restoring the **decorations** and furniture inside the White House. Her objective was to restore them to the way they were when the White House was first built.

Not all additions to the White House have been made in order to save historical objects. Some presidents have made additions to the building just for fun. Over the years, presidents have added a movie theater, a game room, and a bowling alley to the White House.

*In 1962, Jacqueline Kennedy (pictured), wife of President John F. Kennedy, gave the first tour of the White House shown on television.* ▶

In 1948, a bowling alley was built in the White House basement. The bowling alley was put in as a birthday present for President Harry S. Truman (pictured).

In February 2002, the White House was reopened for student tours only. The general public would not be allowed to tour the White House until 2003. Here, Laura Bush, wife of President George W. Bush, greets a student tour.

# The People's House

President Thomas Jefferson first opened the White House to the public in about 1805. Since then, people have enjoyed touring the building and seeing its beautiful rooms and artwork. Today, the White House is the only home of a president or head of state open to the public for free. The only time the White House is closed is during wartime. After **terrorists** attacked New York City and Washington, D.C., on September 11, 2001, the White House was closed to visitors. In 2003, it was reopened to the public. However, only small groups are allowed in.

The White House is more than the president's home and workplace—it is an important part of American history and a symbol of America's place in the world.

*The White House is sometimes called the People's House because it represents America's democratic form of government.*

# Timeline

| | |
|---|---|
| 1791 | President George Washington chooses the location for the capital of the United States of America. |
| 1792 | James Hoban wins contest for best design of the president's home. Construction begins on White House. |
| 1800 | President John Adams moves into the White House. |
| 1812–1815 | The War of 1812 is fought between the United States and England. |
| 1814 | British forces set fire to the White House and other parts of Washington, D.C. |
| 1901 | President Theodore Roosevelt makes White House the official name of the president's home. |
| 1902 | The West Wing is built. |
| 1934 | President Franklin Roosevelt makes the White House larger. |
| 1949 | Reconstruction begins on the inside of the White House. |
| 2001 | Terrorists attack New York City and Washington, D.C. The White House is closed to most of the public for the next two years. |
| 2003 | The White House is reopened to the public. |

# Glossary

**additions** (uh-DISH-uhns) Parts of a building that are added on to the original.

**architect** (AR-ki-tekt) Someone who designs buildings and checks that they are built properly.

**concrete** (KON-kreet) A building material made from a mixture of sand, gravel, cement, and water.

**Congress** (KONG-griss) The government body of the United States that makes laws, made up of the Senate and the House of Representatives.

**contest** (KON-test) A competition.

**decorations** (dek-uh-RAY-shuhnz) Things used to make a room more attractive.

**design** (di-ZINE) To draw something that could be built or made; the shape or style of something.

**invented** (in-VENT-uhd) To have thought up and created something new.

**oval** (OH-vuhl) A shape like an egg.

**restore** (ri-STOR) To bring back to an original condition.

**symbol** (SIM-buhl) A design or an object that represents something else.

**technology** (tek-NOL-uh-jee) The use of science and engineering to do practical things such as make businesses and factories more efficient.

**terrorists** (TER-ur-ists) People who use violence and threats to frighten people into obeying.

# Index

# Primary Sources

**Cover:** The White House [Date Unknown]. **Page 4 (left):** James Hoban [1800]. A wax bas-relief on glass by John Rauschner. White House Historical Association. **Page 4:** Advertisement for Contest to Design the House [March 22, 1792]. *Nation Gazette* (Philadelphia). University of Virginia. **Page 7 (inset):** Letter from John Adams to Abigail Adams [November 2, 1800]. Massachusetts Historical Society. **Page 7:** James Hoban's North Elevation [c.1793]. Maryland Historical Society. **Page 8 (inset):** *The Capture and Burning of Washington by the British, in 1814* [1876]. Wood engraving. Artist Unknown. Library of Congress. **Page 8:** *A view of the President's house in the city of Washington after the conflagration of the 24th Augu 1814* [1814]. An engraving by William Strickland based on a watercolor by George Munger. Library of Congress. **Page 11 (left):** A light fixture converted from gas to electricity [c.1899]. Library of Congress. **Page 11:** Telephones in the White House executive offices [c.1890]. Library of Congress. **Page 12 (top):** President's house (i.e. White House), Washington, D.C., showing south side, probably taken winter [c.1846]. John Plumbe, photographer. Library of Congress. **Page 12:** The completed West Wing [1902]. White House. **Page 15 (left):** Demolition [May 17 1950]. White House Historical Association. **Page 15:** Mr. Truman's Renovation—T White House Is Falling Down [c.1948]. White House Historical Association. **Page 16 (top):** President Bush Hosts Meeting [December 20, 2001]. **Page 16:** President Clinton dancing with his wife, Hillary Rodham Clinton, during the Nationa Governors Association Dinner [February 2, 1997]. Associated Press. **Page 19 (inse** Harry S. Truman Pitching Bowling Ball [April 19, 1948]. Bettmann/ Corbis. **Page 19:** Jackie Kennedy Posing for Film Crew [1962]. Bettmann/Corbis. **Page 20 (inse** Laura Bush Welcomes Tour Group to White House [February 15, 2002]. Getty Images. **Page 20:** White House at Night [Date Unknown].

# Web Sites

Due to the changing nature of Internet links, PowerKids Press has developed an on-line list of Web sites related to the subject of this book. This site is updated regularly. Please use this link to access the list:
http://www.powerkidslinks.com/psas/twh/